HAL LEONARD

GUITAR METHOD

Supplement to Any Guitar Method

EASY POP RHYTHMS

THIRD EDITION

INTRODUCTION

Welcome to *Easy Pop Rhythms*, a collection of 20 pop and rock favorites arranged for easy guitar chord strumming. If you're a beginning guitarist, you've come to the right place. With the songs in this book, you can practice basic chords and strumming patterns—plus learn how to play 20 great tunes!

This book can be used on its own or as a supplement to any guitar method. If you're using it along with the *Hal Leonard Guitar Method*, it coordinates with the skills introduced in Book 1. Use the table of contents on page 3 to see what chords each song contains and to determine when you're ready to play a song.

USING THE AUDIO

This product is available as a book/audio package so you can practice strumming along with a real band. Each song begins with a measure of clicks (or a partial measure, if the song begins with a pickup), which sets the tempo of the song and prepares you for playing along. You may want to practice each song on your own before playing it along with the audio. The strums on each song are patterned after the original recording. Tune your guitar using the tuning notes on the final audio track.

To access audio visit:
www.halleonard.com/mylibrary

Enter Code
8258-7386-7649-8163

ISBN 978-1-4950-9121-6

7777 W. BLUEMOUND RD. P.O. BOX 13819 MILWAUKEE, WI 53213

Visit Hal Leonard Online at
www.halleonard.com

SONG STRUCTURE

The songs in this book have different sections, which may or may not include the following:

Intro
This is usually a short instrumental section that "introduces" the song at the beginning.

Verse
This is one of the main sections of a song and conveys most of the storyline. A song usually has several verses, all with the same music but each with different lyrics.

Chorus
This is often the most memorable section of a song. Unlike the verse, the chorus usually has the same lyrics every time it repeats.

Bridge
This section is a break from the rest of the song, often having a very different chord progression and feel.

Solo
This is an instrumental section, often played over the verse or chorus structure.

Outro
Similar to an intro, this section brings the song to an end.

ENDINGS & REPEATS

Many of the songs have some new symbols that you must understand before playing. Each of these represents a different type of ending.

1st and 2nd Endings
These are indicated by brackets and numbers. The first time through a song section, play the first ending and then repeat. The second time through, skip the first ending, and play through the second ending.

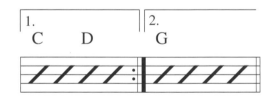

D.S.
This means "Dal Segno" or "from the sign." When you see this abbreviation above the staff, find the sign (𝄋) earlier in the song and resume playing from that point.

al Coda
This means "to the Coda," a concluding section in the song. If you see the words "D.S. al Coda," return to the sign (𝄋) earlier in the song and play until you see the words "To Coda," then skip to the Coda at the end of the song, indicated by the symbol: 𝄌.

al Fine
This means "to the end." If you see the words "D.S. al Fine," return to the sign (𝄋) earlier in the song and play until you see the word "Fine."

D.C.
This means "Da Capo" or "from the head." When you see this abbreviation above the staff, return to the beginning (or "head") of the song and resume playing.

CONTENTS

JAMBALAYA

(On the Bayou)

Words and Music by
Hank Williams

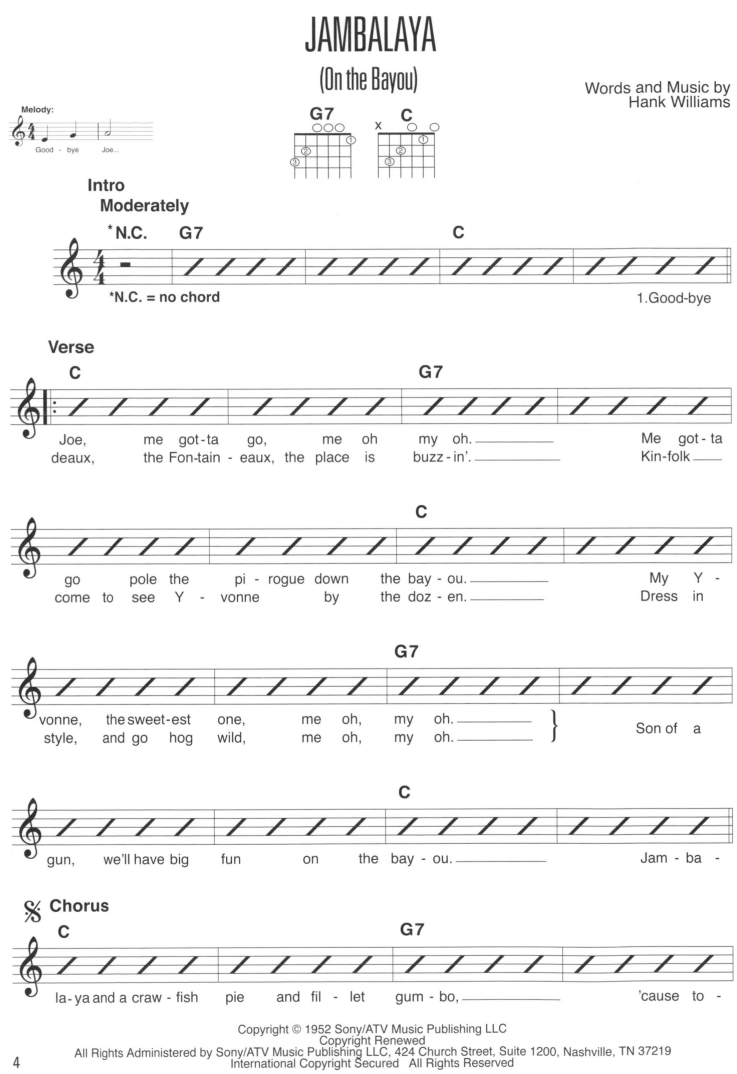

Intro
Moderately

*N.C. = no chord

1.Good-bye

Verse

Joe,   me got-ta go,   me oh   my oh._____   Me got-ta
deaux,   the Fon-tain-eaux, the place is   buzz-in'._____   Kin-folk_____

go   pole the   pi-rogue down   the bay-ou._____   My Y-
come to see Y-vonne   by   the doz-en._____   Dress in

vonne, the sweet-est one,   me oh,   my oh._____   Son of a
style, and go hog wild,   me oh,   my oh._____

gun, we'll have big fun   on   the bay-ou._____   Jam-ba-

𝄋 Chorus

la-ya and a craw-fish pie and fil-let gum-bo,_____   'cause to-

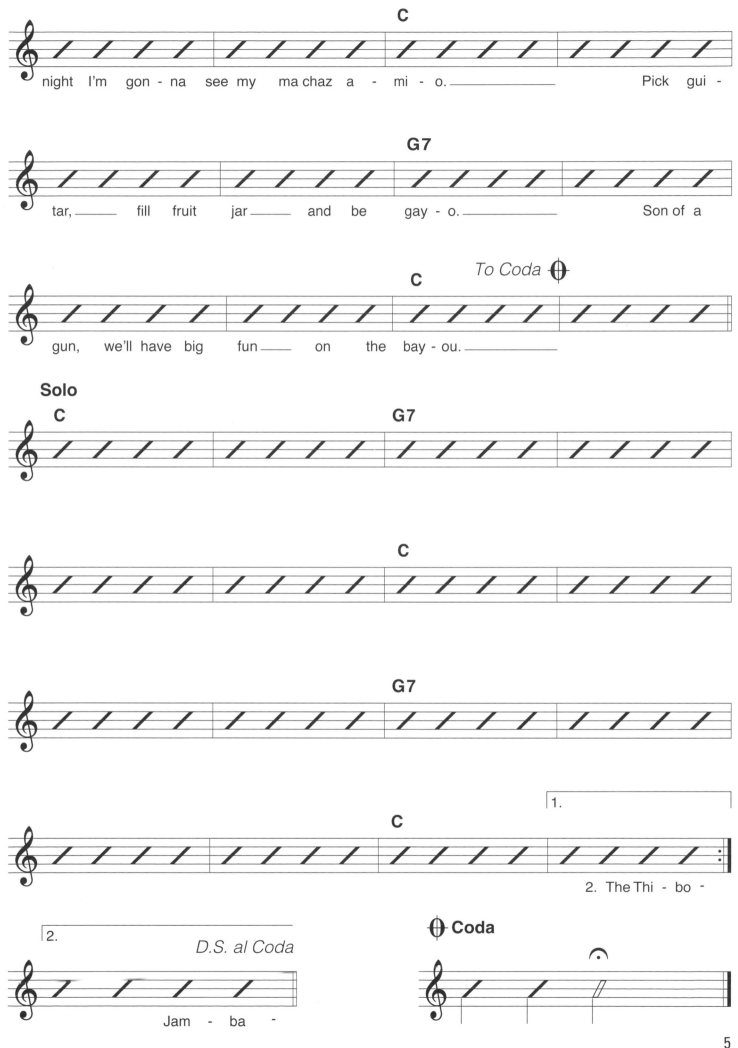

night I'm gon - na see my ma chaz a - mi - o. _____ Pick gui -

C

G7

tar, _____ fill fruit jar _____ and be gay - o. _____ Son of a

To Coda ⊕

C

gun, we'll have big fun _____ on the bay - ou. _____

Solo

C   **G7**

C

G7

1.

C

2. The Thi - bo -

2.

D.S. al Coda

Jam - ba -

⊕ **Coda**

ROCK AROUND THE CLOCK

Words and Music by
Max C. Freedman
and Jimmy DeKnight

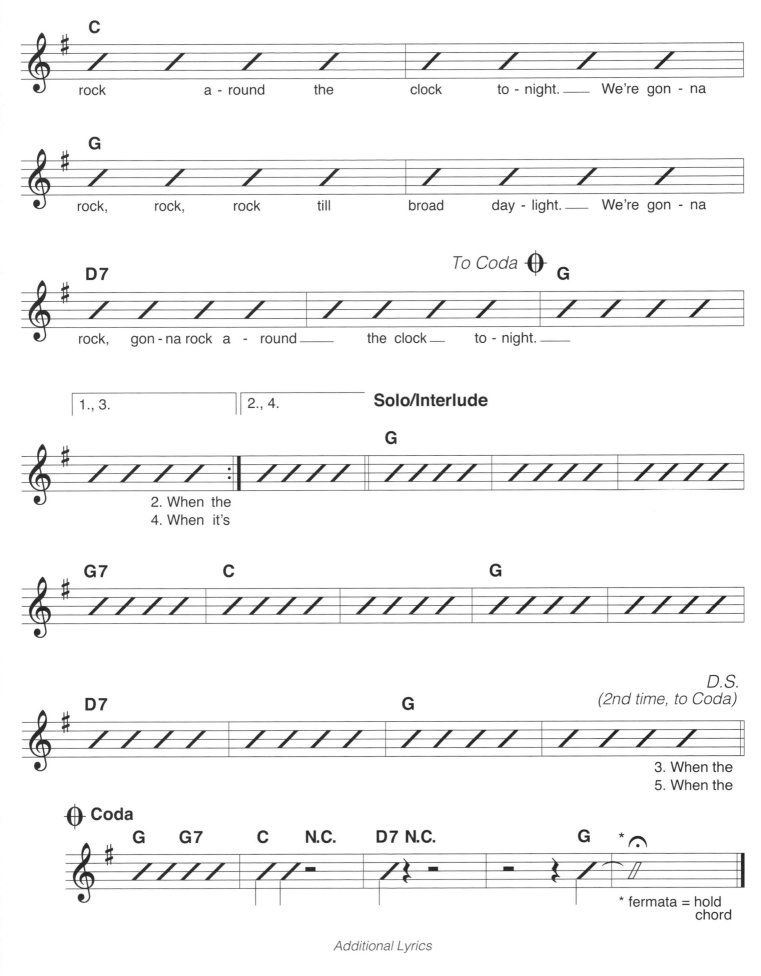

Additional Lyrics

4. When it's eight, nine, ten, eleven too,
   I'll be goin' strong and so will you.
   We're gonna rock around the clock tonight…

5. When the clock strikes twelve, we'll cool off then,
   Start a-rockin' 'round the clock again.
   We're gonna rock around the clock tonight…

WHAT I GOT

BYE BYE LOVE

Words and Music by Felice Bryant
and Boudleaux Bryant

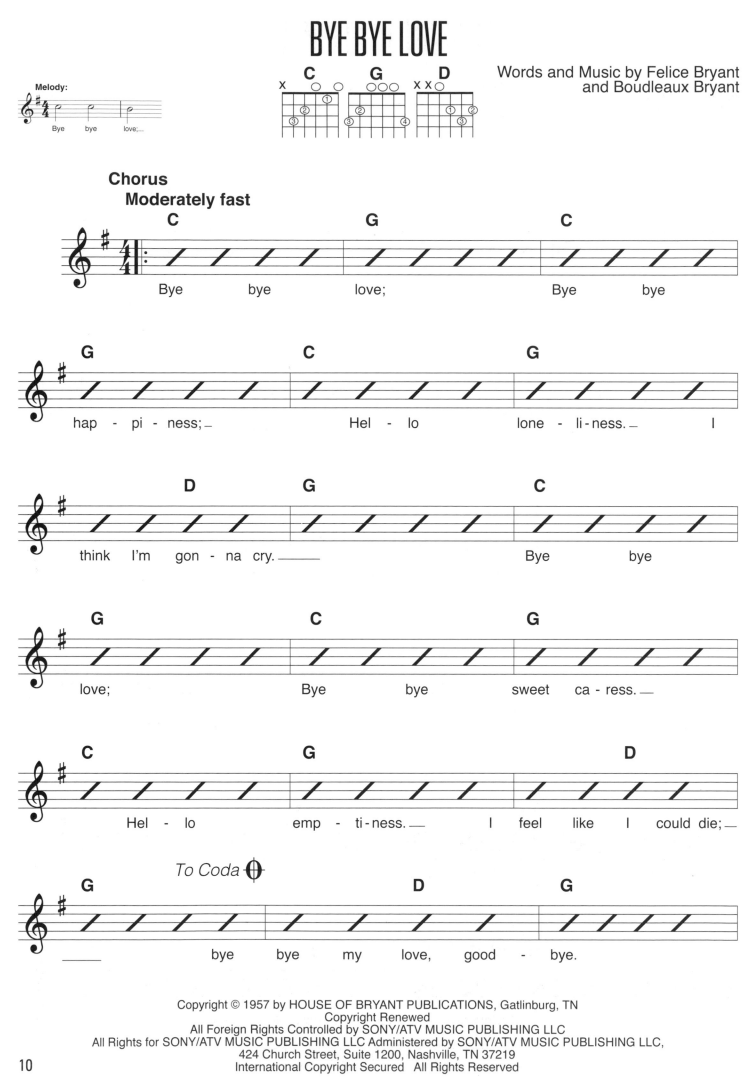

Verse

1. There goes my ba - by ____ with some - one
2. I'm through with ro - mance. ____ I'm through with

new. ____ She sure looks hap - py, ____
love. ____ I'm through with count - ing ____

I sure am blue. ____ She was my
the stars a - bove. ____ And here's the

ba - by ____ till he stepped in; ____
rea - son ____ that I'm so free; ____

____ good - bye to ro - mance ____ that might have
____ my lov - in' ba - by ____ is through with

1.

2.

D.C. al Coda

been. ____
me. ____

Coda
Outro

Repeat and fade

bye my love, good - bye. Bye

LOVE ME DO

Words and Music by John Lennon
and Paul McCartney

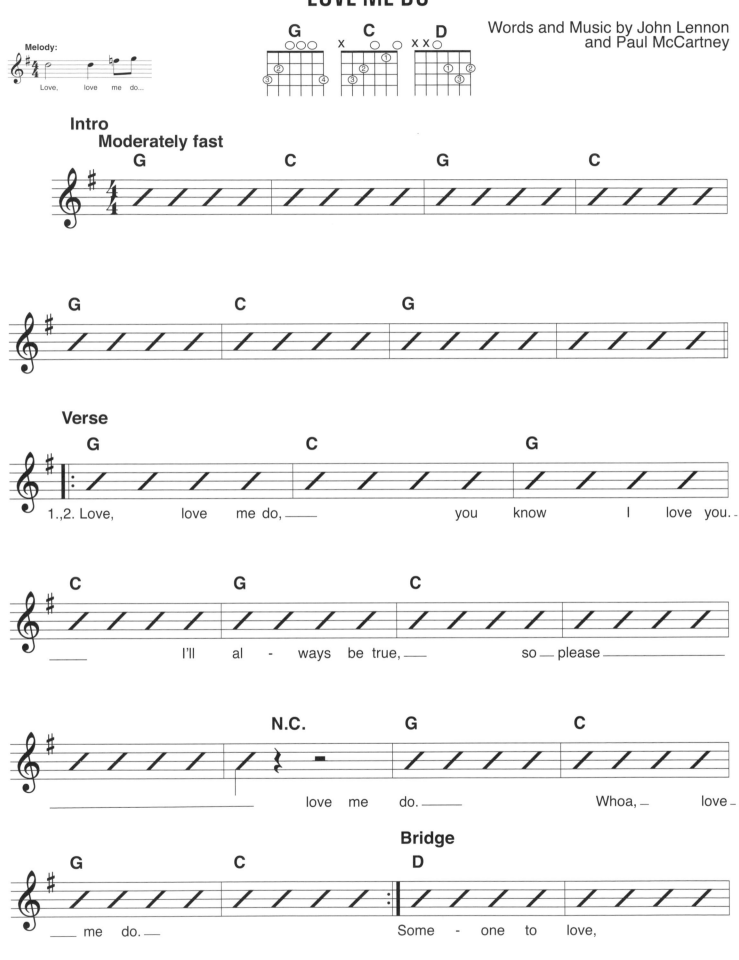

Intro
Moderately fast

Verse

1.,2. Love, love me do, _____ you know I love you. _____ I'll al - ways be true, _____ so — please _____ love me do. _____ Whoa, — love — ___ me do. — Some - one to love,

Bridge

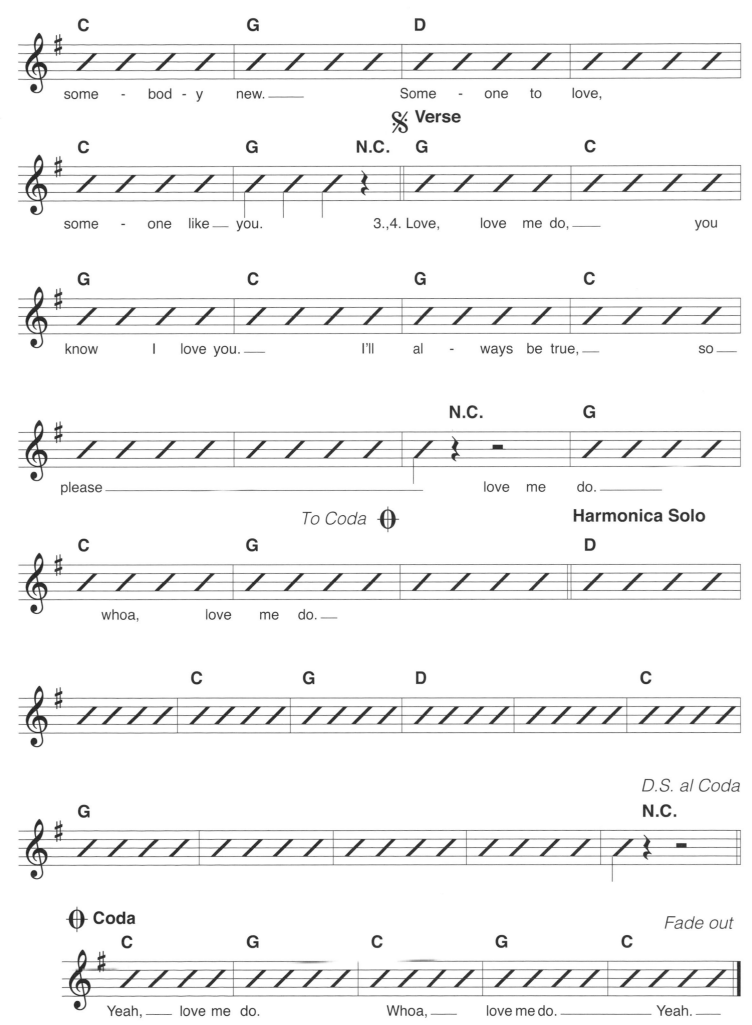

SIMPLE MAN

Words and Music by Ronnie Van Zant
and Gary Rossington

Melody: My ma-ma told me...

% Verse

Moderately slow

1. My mam-ma told me   when I was young,_   "Come sit be-
   time,_   don't live too fast. ___   Trou-bles will
3., 4. *See addditional lyrics*

side _ me   my on-ly son,   and lis-ten
come, ____   and they will pass.   Go find a

close-ly   to what I say. _   And if you
wom-an,   and you'll find love. _   And don't for -

1.
do _ this _ it-'ll help you   some _ sun-ny day."
get, son _ there is some-one   up _

Interlude

2. "Oh, take your
4. "Oh, don't you

Additional Lyrics

3. "Forget your lust for the rich man's gold.
   All that you need is in your soul,
   And you can do this if you try.
   All that I want for you, my son,
   Is to be satisfied."

4. "Oh, don't you worry, you'll find yourself.
   Follow your heart, and nothin' else.
   And you can do this if you try.
   All that I want for you, my son,
   Is to be satisfied."

ALL ALONG THE WATCHTOWER

Words and Music by
Bob Dylan

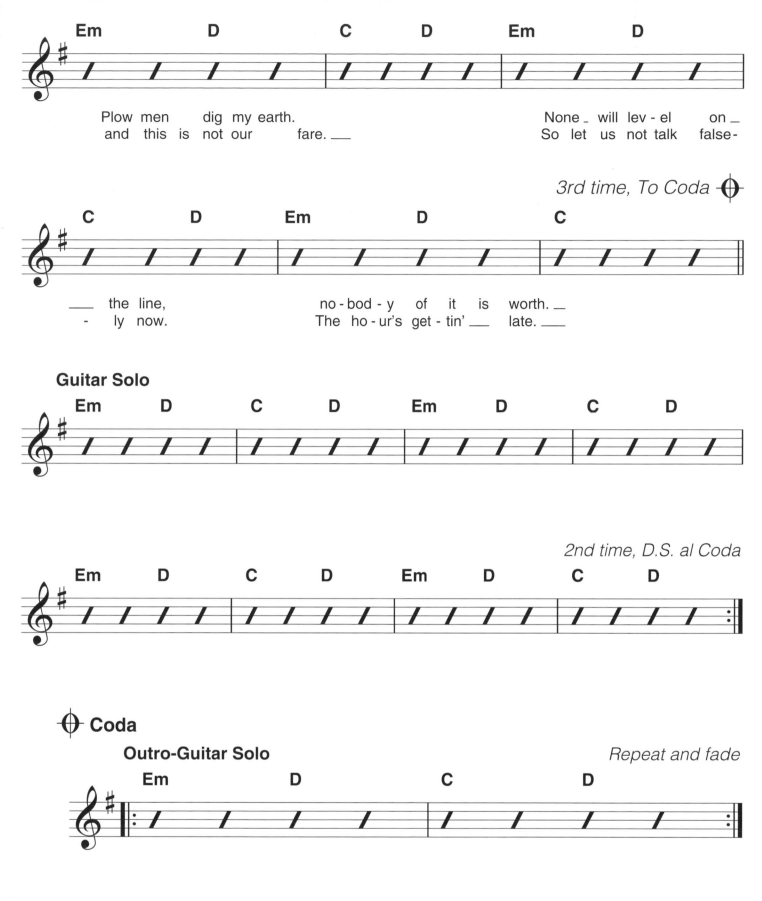

Additional Lyrics

3. Well, all along the watchtower, princes kept the view
   While all the women came and went, barefoot servants, too.
   Outside in the cold distance, a wild cat did growl.
   Two riders were approachin', and the wind began to howl.

WONDERFUL TONIGHT

Words and Music by
Eric Clapton

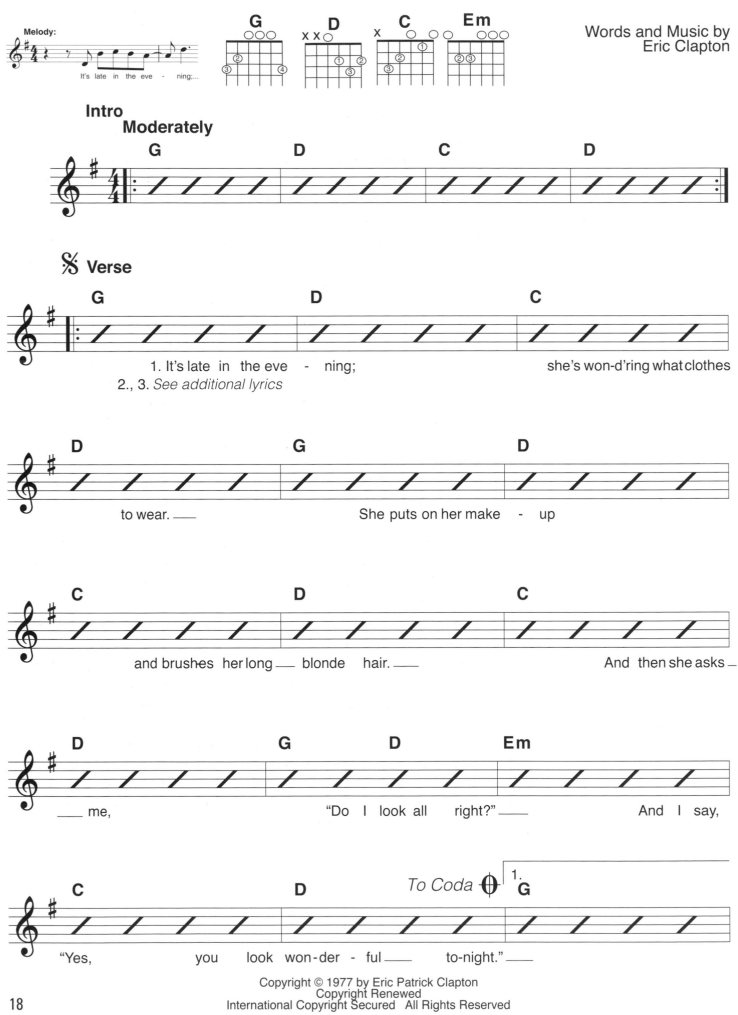

Melody:

It's late in the eve - ning;...

Intro **Moderately**

G   D   C   D

%　**Verse**

G   D   C

1. It's late in the eve - ning;   she's won-d'ring what clothes
2., 3. *See additional lyrics*

D   G   D

to wear. ___   She puts on her make - up

C   D   C

and brushes her long ___ blonde hair. ___   And then she asks

D   G   D   Em

___ me,   "Do I look all   right?" ___   And I say,

C   D   *To Coda* ⊕   1. G

"Yes,   you look won - der - ful ___ to - night." ___

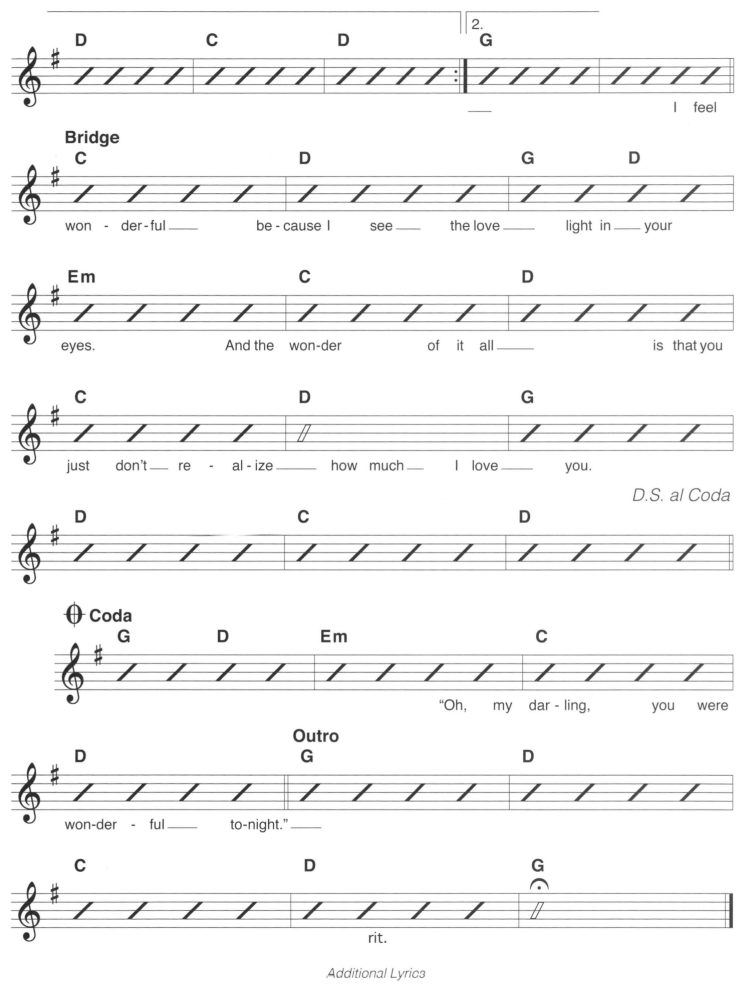

Bridge

won - der-ful —— be - cause I see —— the love —— light in —— your

eyes. And the won - der of it all —— is that you

just don't —— re - al - ize —— how much —— I love —— you.

D.S. al Coda

Coda

"Oh, my dar - ling, you were

Outro

won-der - ful —— to-night." ——

rit.

Additional Lyrics

2. We go to a party, and ev'ryone turns to see
   This beautiful lady that's walking around with me.
   And then she asks me, "Do you feel alright?"
   And I say, "Yes, I feel wonderful tonight."

3. It's time to go home now, and I've got an aching head.
   So I give her the car keys and she helps me to bed.
   And then I tell her, as I turn out the light,
   I say, "My darling, you were wonderful tonight."

WAGON WHEEL

Words and Music by
Bob Dylan and Ketch Secor

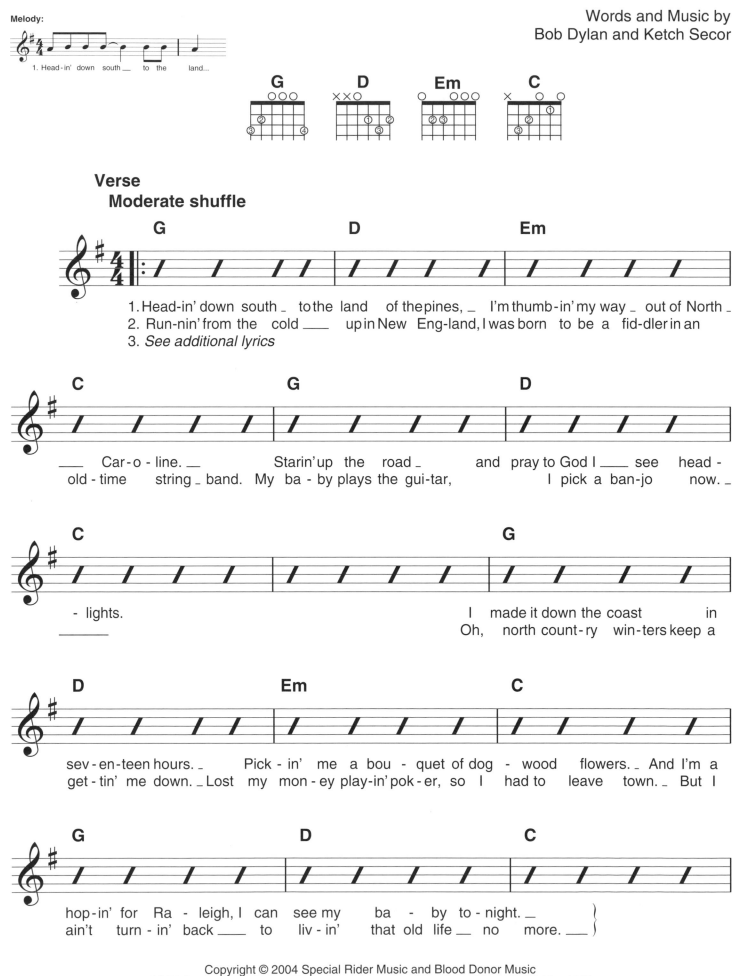

Verse
Moderate shuffle

1. Head-in' down south _ to the land of the pines, _ I'm thumb-in' my way _ out of North _
2. Run-nin' from the cold ___ up in New Eng-land, I was born to be a fid-dler in an
3. *See additional lyrics*

___ Car-o-line. _ Starin' up the road _ and pray to God I ___ see head-
old-time string _ band. My ba-by plays the gui-tar, I pick a ban-jo now. _

- lights.
_____ Oh, north count-ry win-ters keep a

I made it down the coast in

sev-en-teen hours. _ Pick-in' me a bou-quet of dog-wood flowers. _ And I'm a
get-tin' me down. _ Lost my mon-ey play-in' pok-er, so I had to leave town. But I

hop-in' for Ra-leigh, I can see my ba-by to-night. _
ain't turn-in' back ___ to liv-in' that old life _ no more. ___

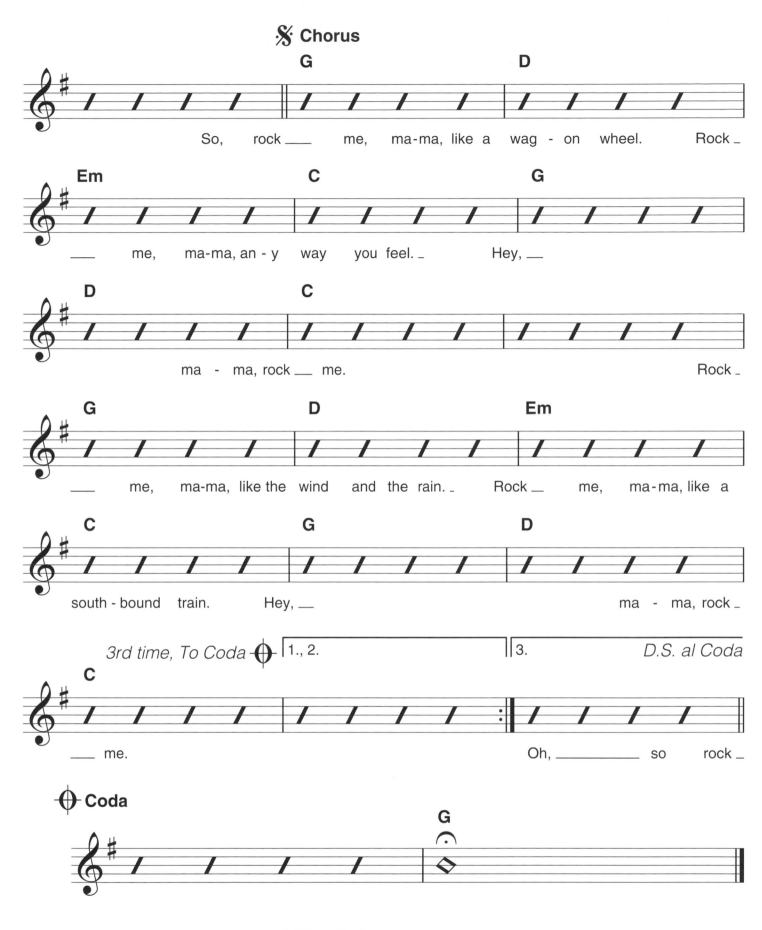

3rd time, To Coda

D.S. al Coda

Additional Lyrics

3. Walkin' through the South out of Roanoke,
I caught a trucker out of Philly, had a nice long toke.
But he's a headin' west from the Cumberland Gap to Johnson City, Tennessee.
I got, I gotta move on before the sun.
I hear my baby callin' my name and I know that she's the only one.
And if I die in Raleigh, at least I will die free.

TEACH YOUR CHILDREN

Words and Music by
Graham Nash

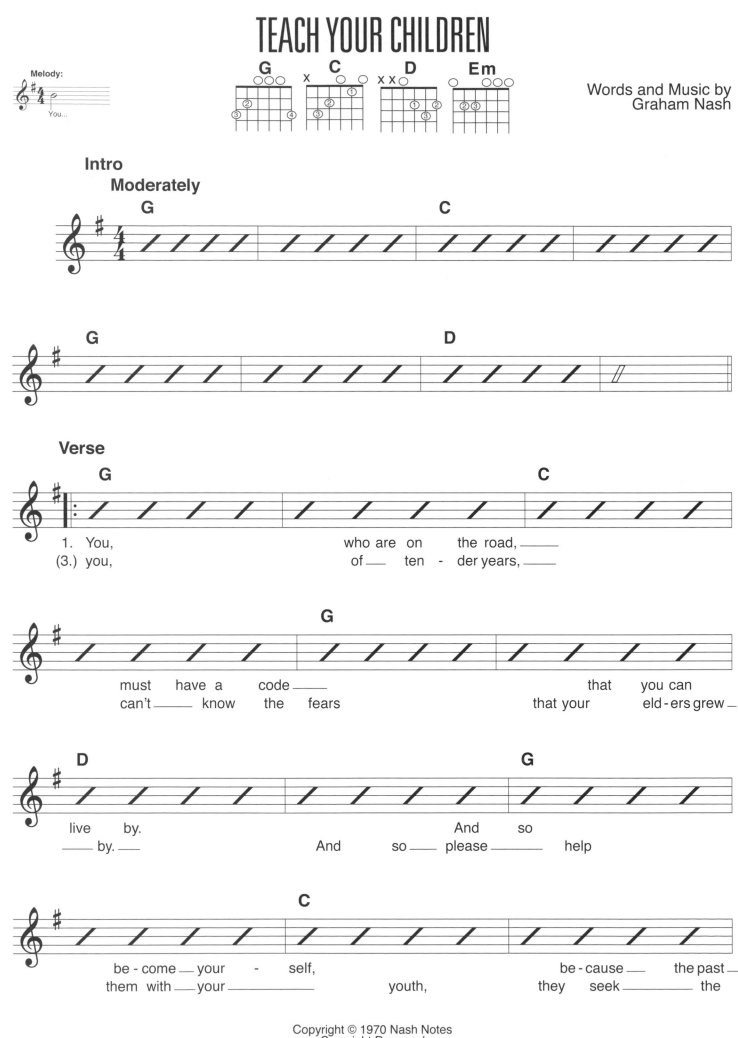

Intro
Moderately

Verse

1. You,   who are on   the road, _____
(3.) you,   of ___ ten - der years, _____

must   have a   code _____   that   you can
can't ___ know   the   fears   that your   eld - ers grew _____

live   by.   And   so
___ by. ___   And   so ___ please _____ help

be - come ___ your - self,   be - cause ___ the past
them with ___ your _____   youth,   they   seek _____ the

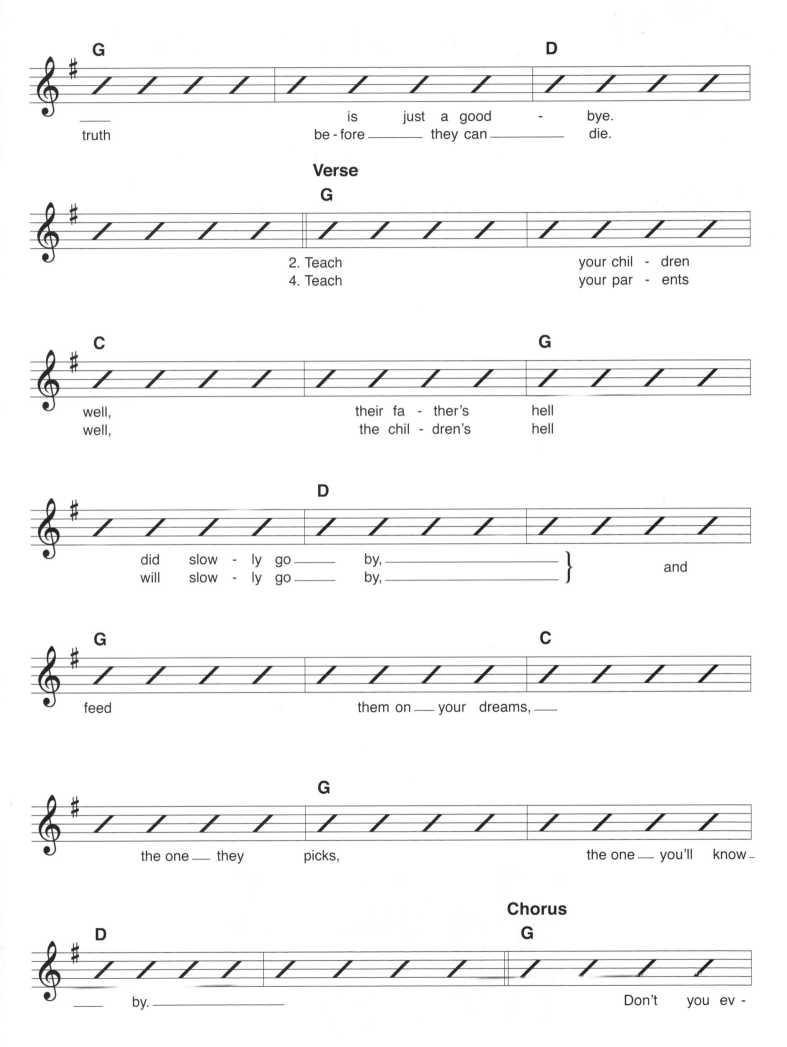

- er ask — them why, if they told you, you — would

cry, so just look at them — and sigh, —

and know they

Interlude/Outro

love — you.

1.

2.

3. And

NO WOMAN NO CRY

Words and Music by
Vincent Ford

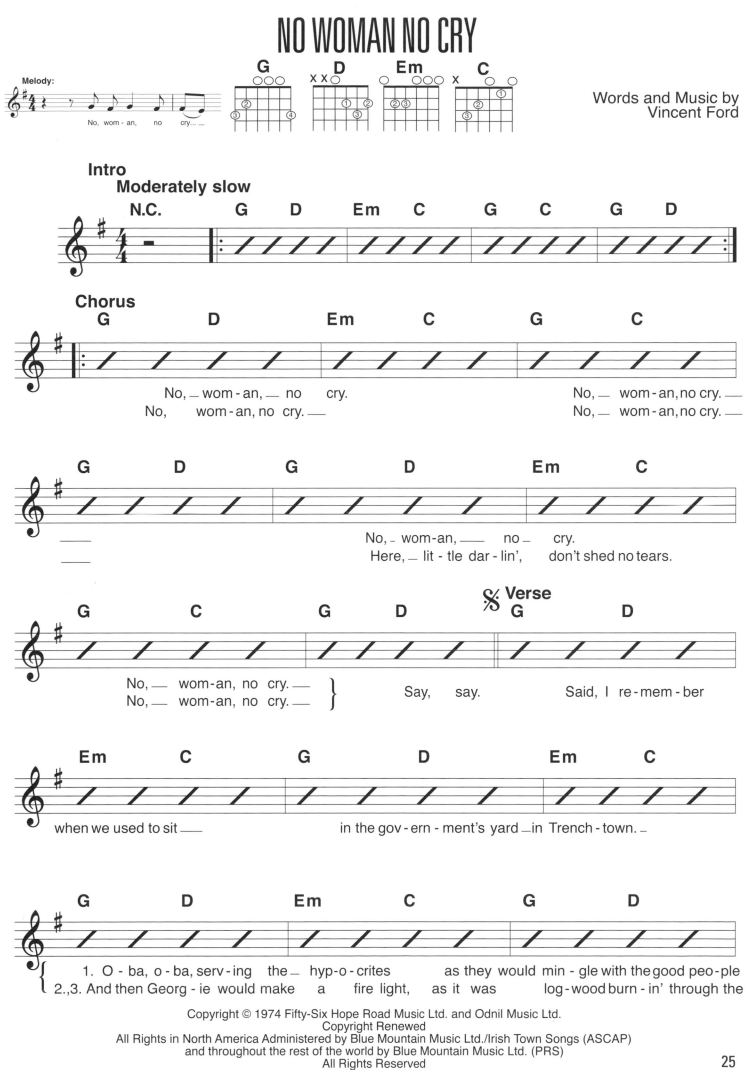

we meet. / night.

Good friends we had, — oh good friends we've lost —
Then we would cook corn - meal por - ridge, —

a - long — the way. — / of which I'll share — with you. —

In this bright - fu - ture, you —
My feet — is my

To Coda ⊕

— can't for - get your past. / on - ly car - riage. ——

So dry your tears — I — say. And
So I've got to push on through. But while I'm gone, I mean-a...

Bridge

Ev-'ry-thing is gon-na be — al - right. Ev - 'ry - thing's gon-na be al - right.

Ev-'ry-thing is gon-na be al - right. Ev - 'ry - thing's gon - na be — alright. { I say, So,

Chorus

wom - an, no cry. No, no wom - an, — wom - an no cry. —

Oh, my lit-tle sis - ter, don't shed no tears. —

LEARNING TO FLY

Words and Music by Tom Petty
and Jeff Lynne

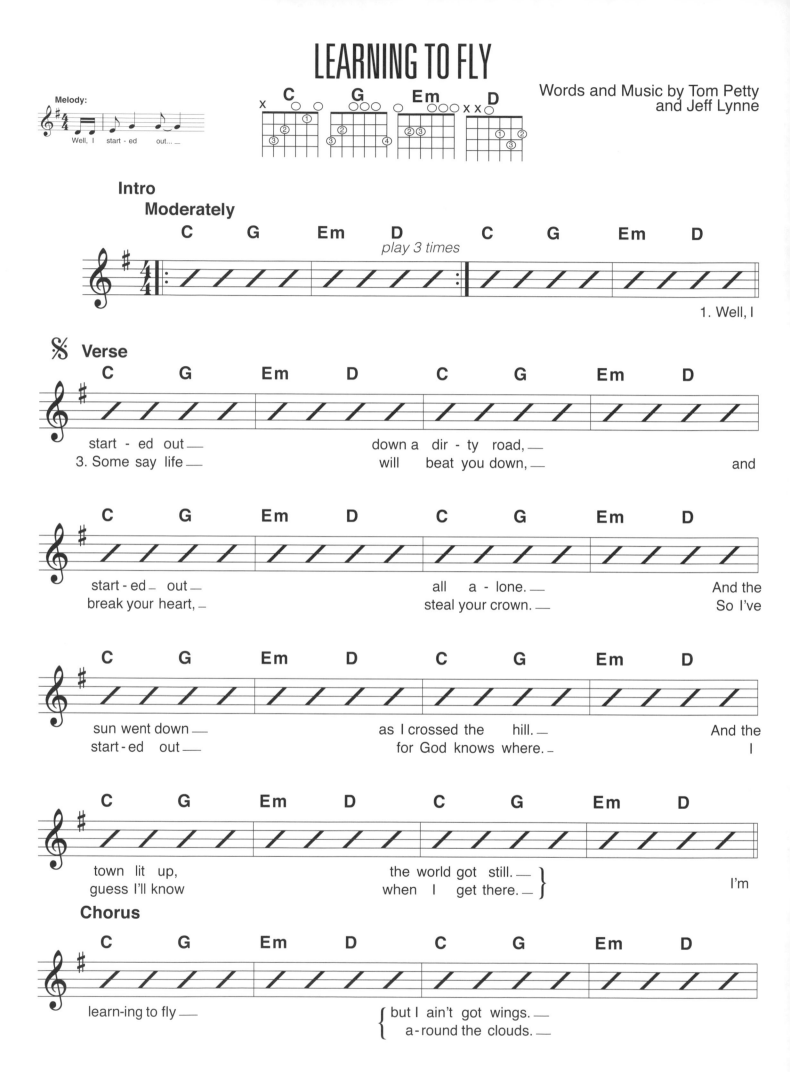

Intro
Moderately

play 3 times

1. Well, I

Verse

start - ed out ___ down a dir - ty road, ___ and
3. Some say life ___ will beat you down, ___

start - ed ___ out ___ all a - lone. ___ And the
break your heart, ___ steal your crown. ___ So I've

sun went down ___ as I crossed the hill. ___ And the
start - ed out ___ for God knows where. ___ I

town lit up, ___ the world got still. ___ I'm
guess I'll know ___ when I get there. ___

Chorus

learn-ing to fly ___ { but I ain't got wings. ___
{ a-round the clouds. ___

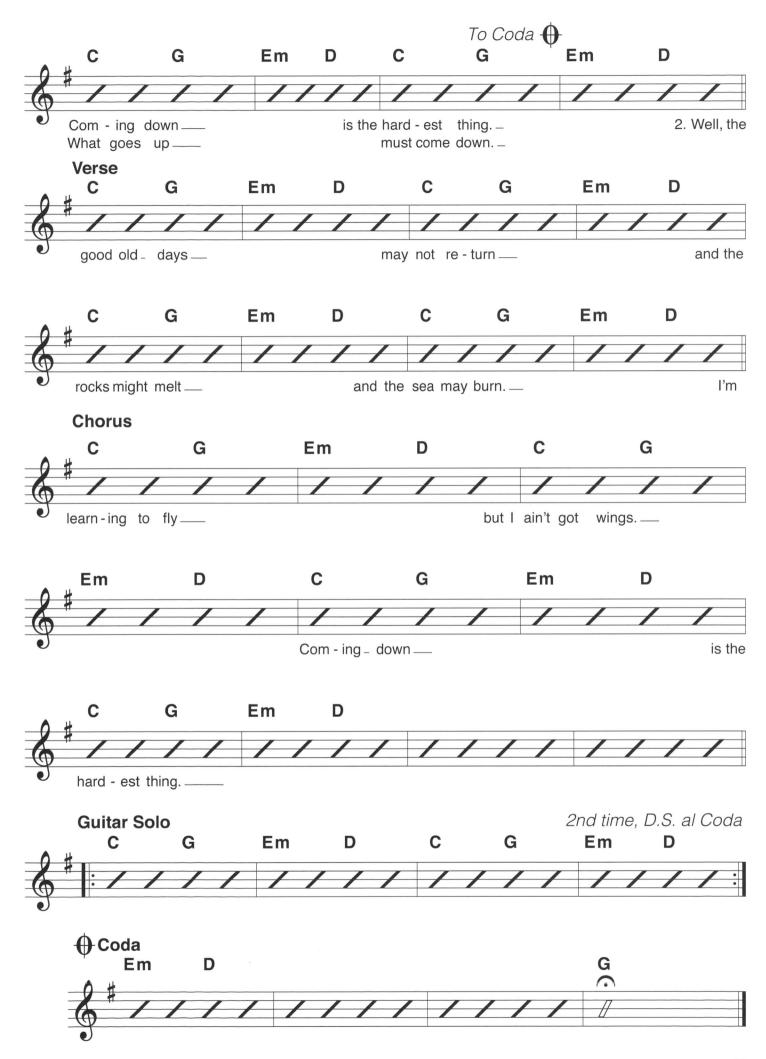

BROWN EYED GIRL

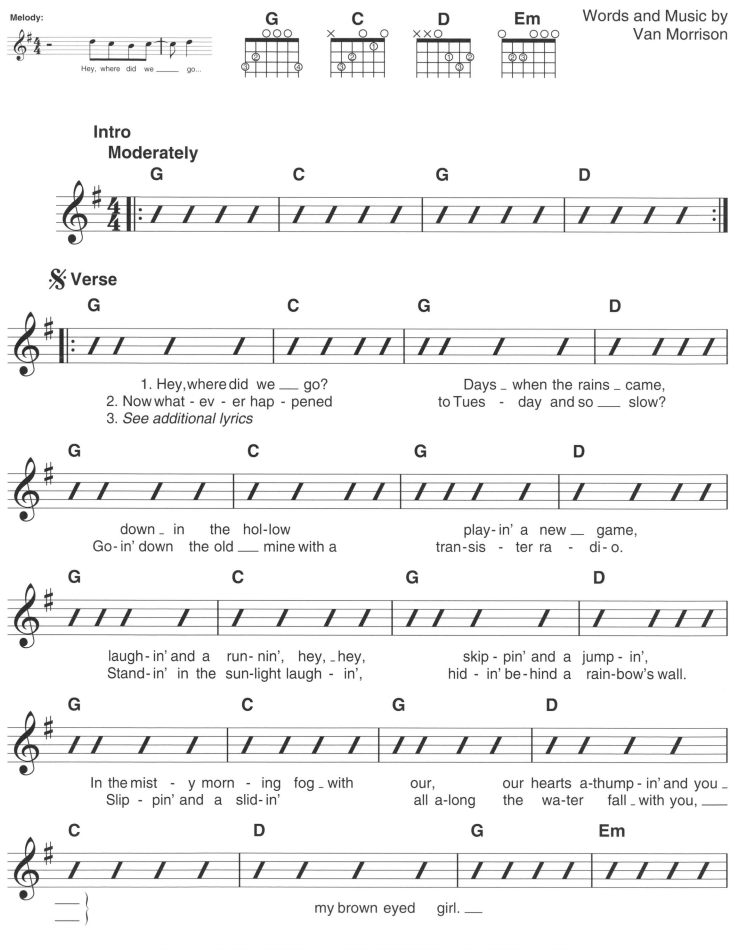

Words and Music by
Van Morrison

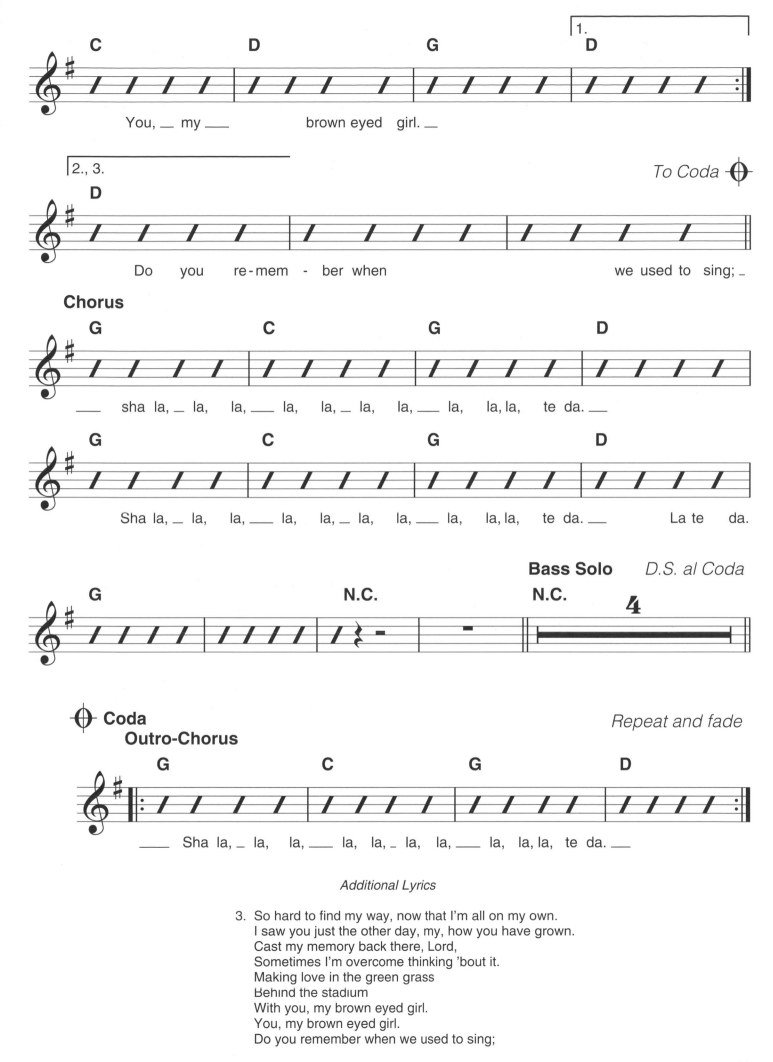

Additional Lyrics

3. So hard to find my way, now that I'm all on my own.
   I saw you just the other day, my, how you have grown.
   Cast my memory back there, Lord,
   Sometimes I'm overcome thinking 'bout it.
   Making love in the green grass
   Behind the stadium
   With you, my brown eyed girl.
   You, my brown eyed girl.
   Do you remember when we used to sing;

HEY, SOUL SISTER

Words and Music by Pat Monahan,
Espen Lind and Amund Bjorklund

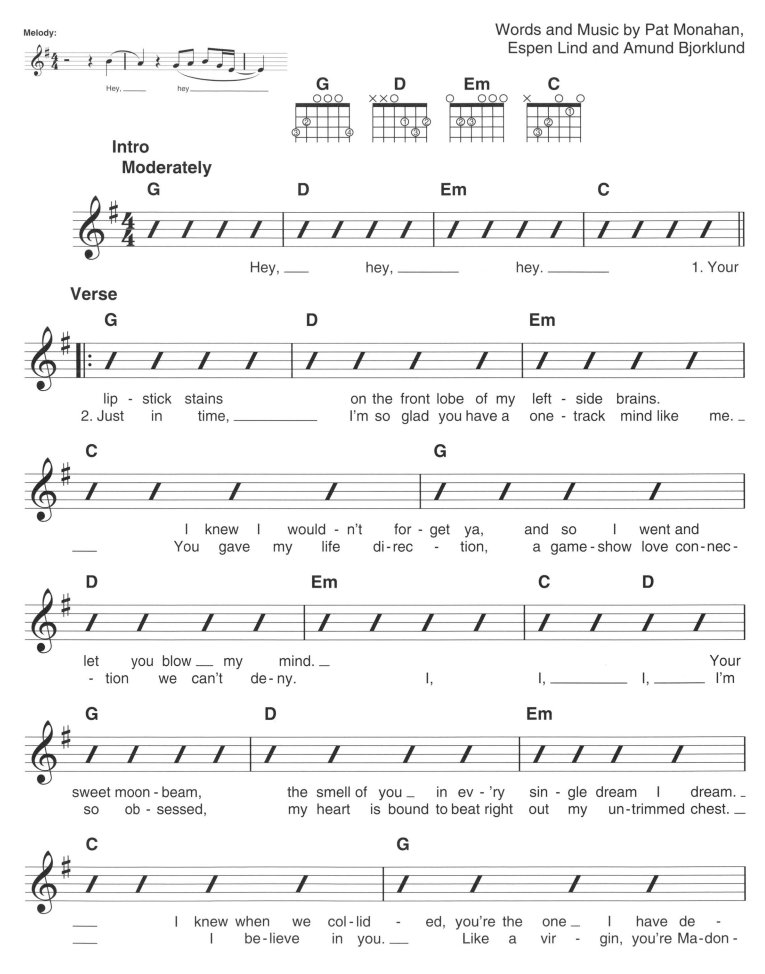

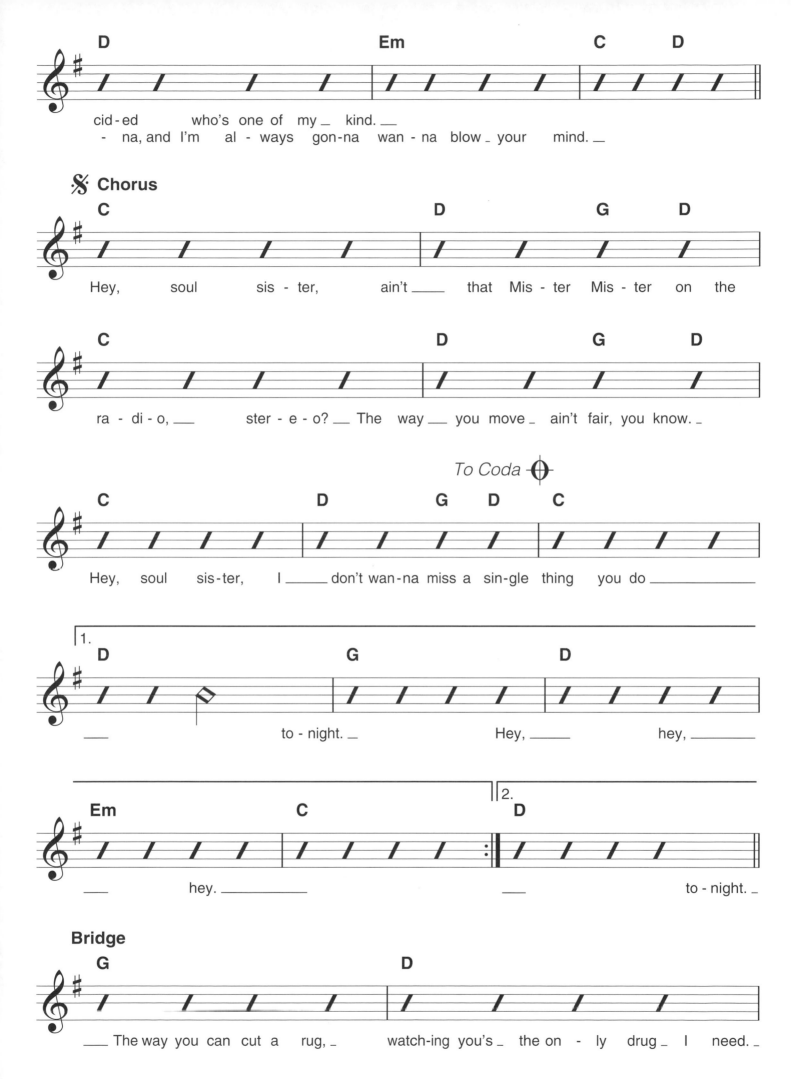

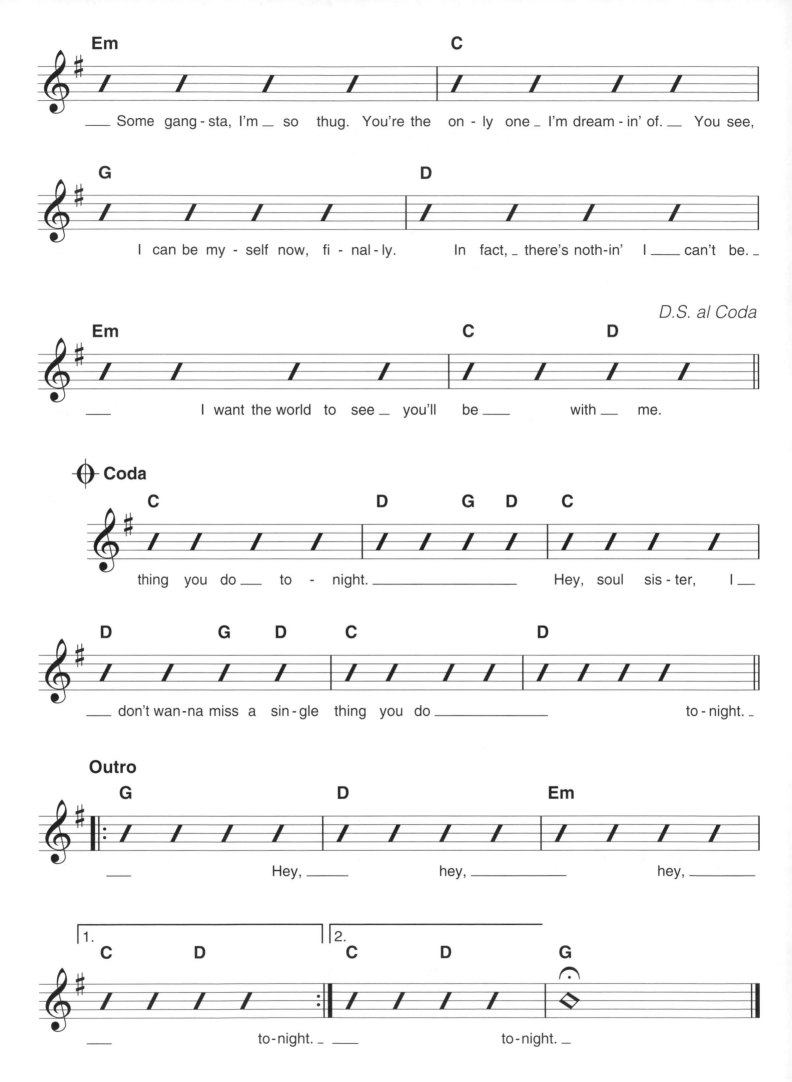

IRIS
from the Motion Picture CITY OF ANGELS

Words and Music by
John Rzeznik

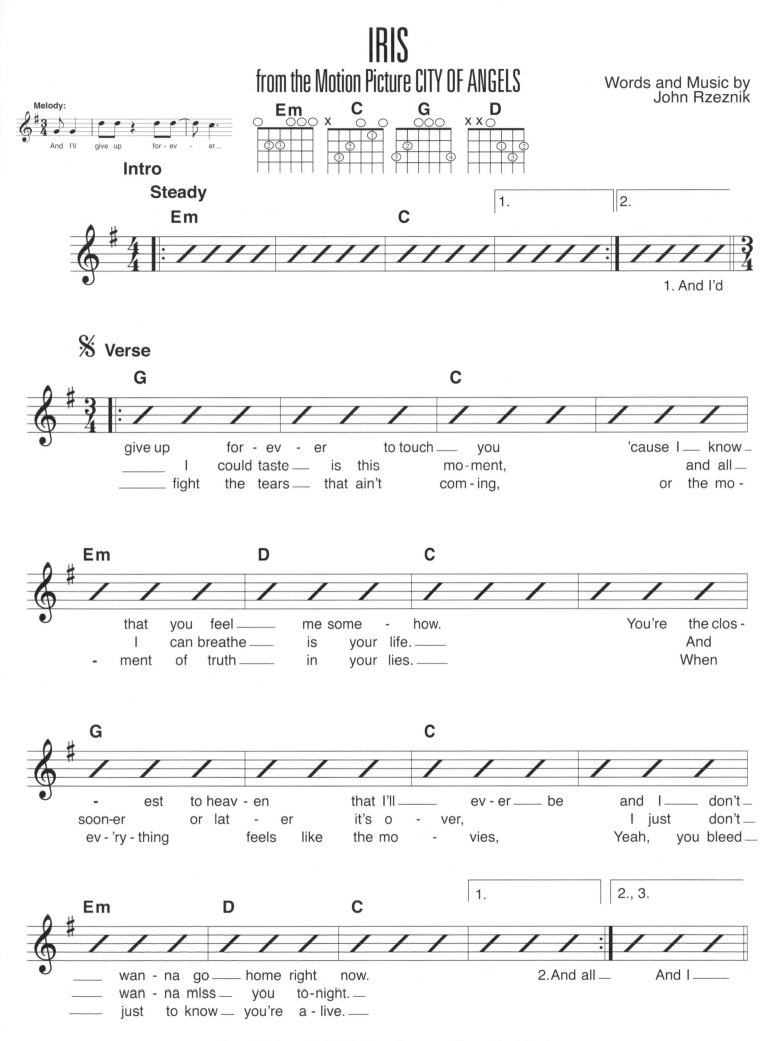

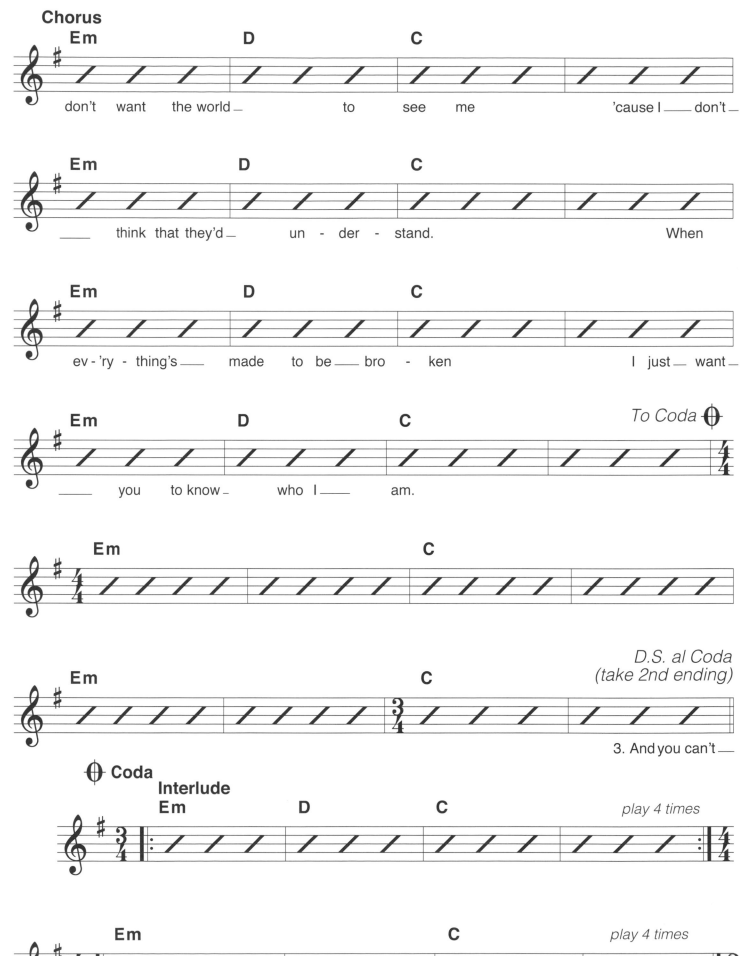

Chorus

Em · · · / D · · · / C · · · / · · · ·

don't want the world — to see me 'cause I — don't —

Em · · · / D · · · / C · · · / · · · ·

— think that they'd — un - der - stand. When

Em · · · / D · · · / C · · · / · · · ·

ev - 'ry - thing's — made to be — bro - ken I just — want —

Em · · · / D · · · / C · · · / · · · · *To Coda* ⊕

— you to know — who I — am.

Em · · · / · · · / C · · · / · · · ·

*D.S. al Coda
(take 2nd ending)*

Em · · · / · · · / C · · · / · · · ·

3. And you can't —

⊕ **Coda**
Interlude

Em · · · / D · · · / C · · · / · · · · *play 4 times*

Em · · · / · · · / C · · · / · · · · *play 4 times*

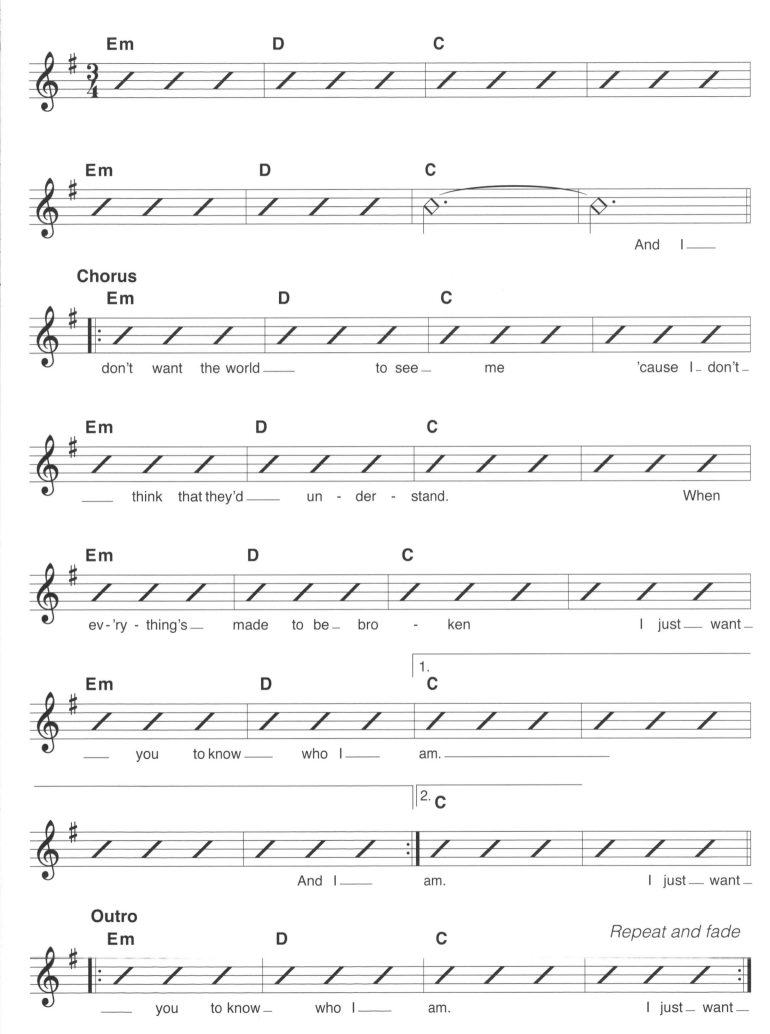

ALL APOLOGIES

Words and Music by
Kurt Cobain

SURFIN' U.S.A.

Words and Music by
Chuck Berry

TWIST AND SHOUT

Words and Music by Bert Russell
and Phil Medley

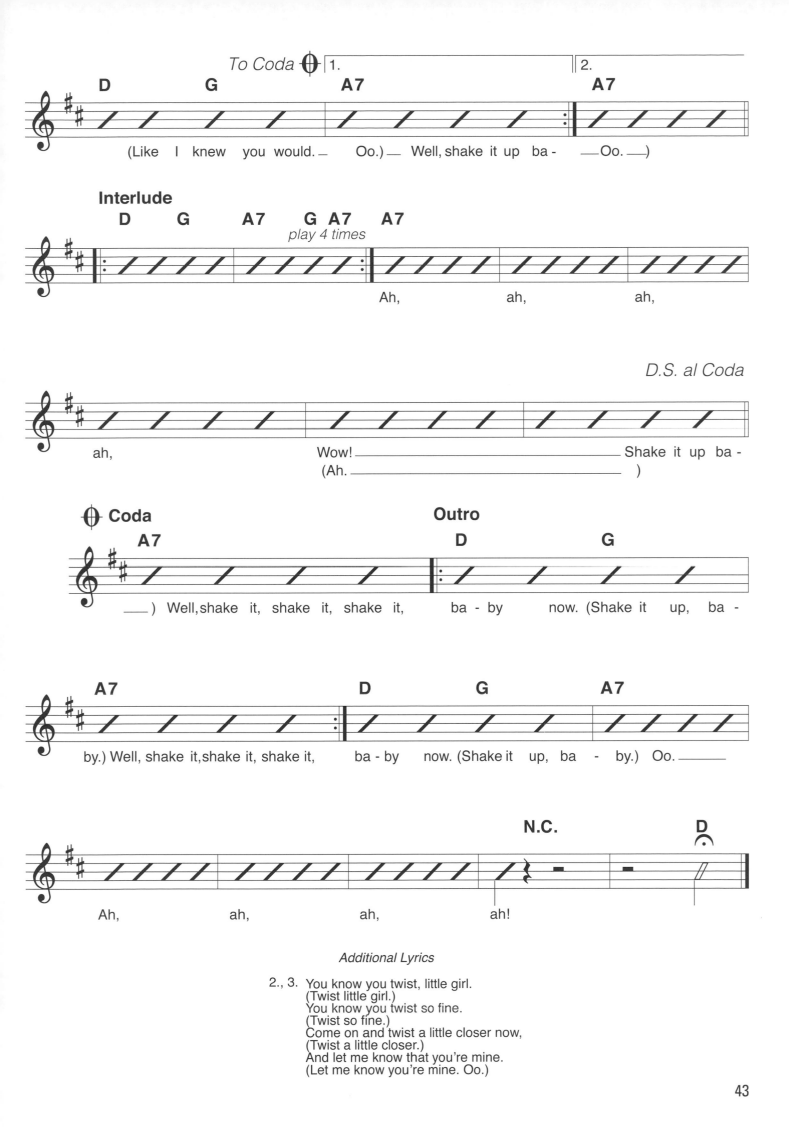

Additional Lyrics

2., 3. You know you twist, little girl.
(Twist little girl.)
You know you twist so fine.
(Twist so fine.)
Come on and twist a little closer now,
(Twist a little closer.)
And let me know that you're mine.
(Let me know you're mine. Oo.)

THAT'LL BE THE DAY

Words and Music by Jerry Allison,
Norman Petty and Buddy Holly

Intro
Moderately

N.C.

D7

Chorus

C

Well, _____ that - 'll be the day when

G

you say good-bye, yes, that - 'll be the day when you make me cry - y. You

C   **G**

say you're gon-na leave; you know it's a lie, — 'cause that - 'll be the day _____

Verse

D7   **G**   **C**   **G**

when I die.
  1. Well, you give me all your lov - in' and your tur - tle dov - in', a -
  2. Well, uh, when Cu - pid shot his dart, he shot it at your heart.

C   **G**   **C**

all your hugs and kiss-es and your mon - ey, too. — Well, - uh, y' know you love me, ba - by.
So if we ever part then I'll leave you. You sit and hold me and you

G   **A7**   **D7**

Still _____ you tell me may - be that some - day, well, I'll be blue. Well,
tell _____ me bold - ly

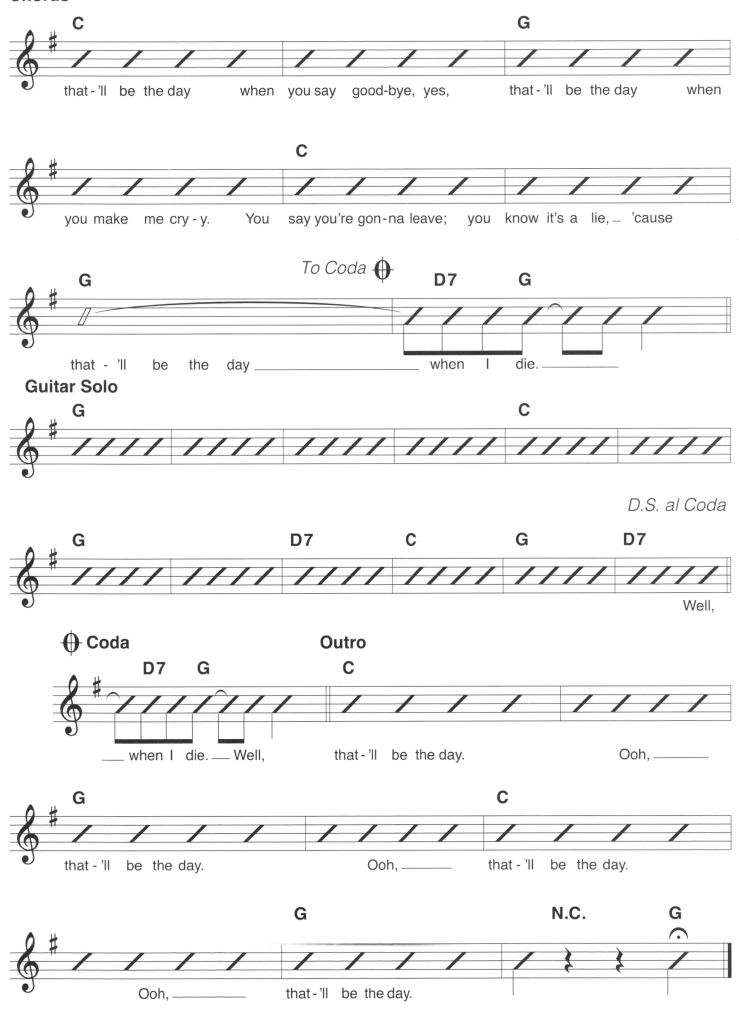

DON'T BE CRUEL
(To a Heart That's True)

Words and Music by Otis Blackwell
and Elvis Presley

STRUM PATTERNS

The first responsibility of a chord player is to *play the right chord on time*. Keep this in mind as you learn new strumming patterns. No matter how concerned you might be with right-hand strumming, getting to the correct chord with your left hand is more important. If necessary, leave the old chord early in order to arrive at the new chord on time.

That said, here are some suggested strum patterns. Choose one that challenges you, and practice it. Whenever you learn a new chord or progression, try putting it into one of these patterns. Also, try applying these to the songs in this book.

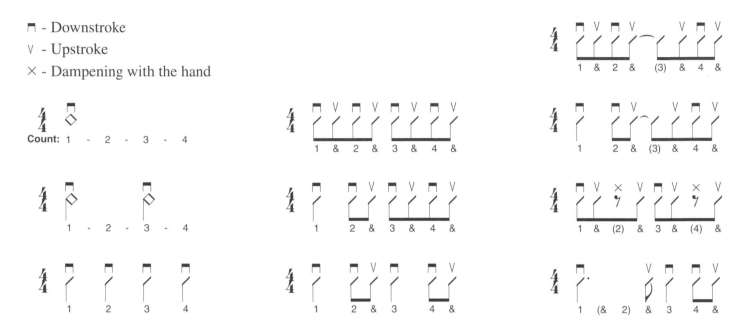

Eighth notes in the above strums may be played even or uneven ("swung") depending on the style of music.

CHORDS

Here are all the chords needed to play the songs in this book.

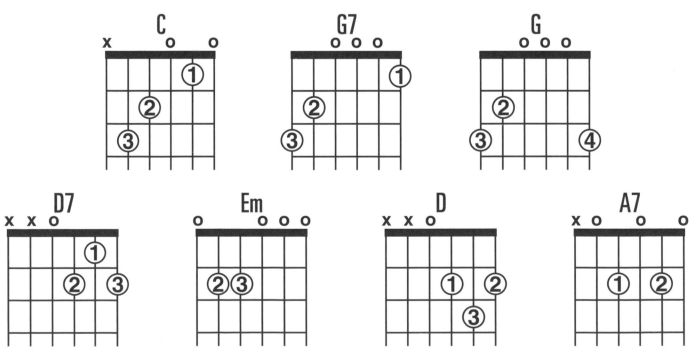

These are presented in the order you learned them in Book 1 of the *Hal Leonard Guitar Method*.